tourism TATTLER

Issue 12 (DECEMBER) 2015

PUBLISHER
Tourism Tattler (Pty) Ltd.
PO Box 891, Umhlanga Rocks, 4320
KwaZulu-Natal, South Africa.
Website: www.tourismtattler.com

EXECUTIVE EDITOR Des Langkilde
Cell: +27 (0)82 374 7260
Fax: +27 (0)86 651 8080
E-mail: editor@tourismtattler.com
Skype: tourismtattler

MAGAZINE ADVERTISING
ADVERTISING DIRECTOR Bev Langkilde
Cell: +27 (0)71 224 9971
Fax: +27 (0)86 656 3860
E-mail: bev@tourismtattler.com
Skype: bevtourismtattler

SUBSCRIPTIONS
http://eepurl.com/bocldD

BACK ISSUES (Click on the covers below).

▼ Nov 2015   ▼ Oct 2015   ▼ Sep 2015

▼ Aug 2015   ▼ Jul 2015   ▼ Jun 2015

▼ May 2015   ▼ Apr 2015   ▼ Mar 2015

▼ Feb 2015   ▼ Jan 2015   ▼ Dec 2014

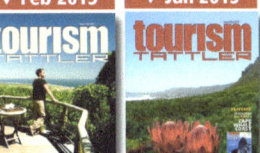

Contents

I0472727

11 CONSERVATION: The Hawking Centre Supports VulPro.

12 CONSERVATION: Diani Beach - Magical Kenya's Hidden Gem.

18 HOSPITALITY: Property Review - Alfajiri Villas, Kenya.

IN THIS ISSUE

EDITORIAL CONTRIBUTORS

Adv. Louis Nel
Des Langkilde

Dr. Peter E. Tarlow
Kerri Wolter

Kirsty Coetzee
Unathi Henama

MAGAZINE SPONSORS

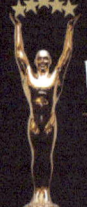

PROMOTING TOURISM TO
AFRICA
FROM ALL CORNERS OF THE WORLD

Recognised as the Voice of African Tourism, Atta reaches across 22 countries in Africa, showcasing over 530 elite buyers and suppliers of African tourism product.

- Leading role at trade shows around the world
- Networking opportunities
- Industry representation on international commitees & the media
- Interactive platform for information & education
- Daily news service on all aspects of African tourism
- Network of specialist consultants

Join our knowledgeable and experienced membership to increase awareness and visibility of your company

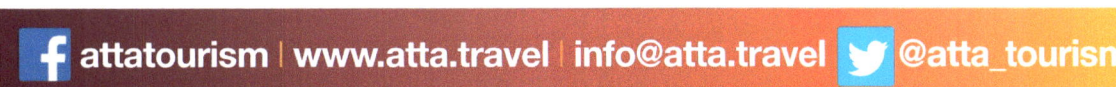

f attatourism | **www.atta.travel** | **info@atta.travel** | 🐦 **@atta_tourism**

Lead Sponsor | Working in partnership with Atta

SOUTH AFRICAN AIRWAYS

A STAR ALLIANCE MEMBER

Accreditation

Official Travel Trade Journal and Media Partner to:

The Africa Travel Association (ATA)

Tel: +1 212 447 1357 • Email: info@africatravelassociation.org • Website: www.africatravelassociation.org

ATA is a registered non-profit trade association in the USA, with headquarters in New York and chapters around the world. ATA is dedicated to promoting travel and tourism to Africa and strengthening intra-Africa partnerships. Established in 1975, ATA provides services to both the public and private sectors of the industry. ATA's annual events in the USA and Africa bring industry professionals together to shape Africa's tourism agenda.

The African Travel & Tourism Association (Atta)

Tel: +44 20 7937 4408 • Email: info@atta.travel • Website: www.atta.travel

Members in 22 African countries and 37 worldwide use Atta to: Network and collaborate with peers in African tourism; Grow their online presence with a branded profile; Ask and answer specialist questions and give advice; and Attend key industry events.

National Accommodation Association of South Africa (NAA-SA)

Tel: +2786 186 2272 • Fax: +2786 225 9858 • Website: www.naa-sa.co.za

The NAA-SA is a network of mainly smaller accommodation providers around South Africa – from B&Bs in country towns offering comfortable personal service to luxurious boutique city lodges with those extra special touches – you're sure to find a suitable place, and at the same time feel confident that your stay at an NAA-SA member's establishment will meet your requirements.

Regional Tourism Organisation of Southern Africa (RETOSA)

Tel: +2711 315 2420/1 • Fax: +2711 315 2422 • Website: www.retosa.co.za

RETOSA is a Southern African Development Community (SADC) institution responsible for tourism growth and development. RETOSA's aims are to increase tourist arrivals to the region through. RETOSA Member States are Angola, Botswana, DR Congo, Lesotho, Madagascar, Malawi, Mauritius, Mozambique, Namibia, Seychelles, South Africa, Swaziland, Tanzania, Zambia and Zimbabwe.

Southern Africa Tourism Services Association (SATSA)

Tel: +2786 127 2872 • Fax: +2711 886 755 • Website: www.satsa.com

SATSA is a credibility accreditation body representing the private sector of the inbound tourism industry. SATSA members are Bonded thus providing a financial guarantee against advance deposits held in the event of the involuntary liquidation. SATSA represents: Transport providers, Tour Operators, DMC's, Accommodation Suppliers, Tour Brokers, Adventure Tourism Providers, Business Tourism Providers and Allied Tourism Services providers.

Southern African Vehicle Rental and Leasing Association (SAVRALA)

Contact: manager@savrala.co.za • Website: w

Founded in the 1970's, SAVRALA is the representative voice of Southern Africa's vehicle rental, leasing and fleet management sector. Our members have a combined national footprint with more than 600 branches countrywide. SAVRALA are instrumental in steering industry standards and continuously strive to protect both their members' interests, and those of the public, and are therefore widely respected within corporate and government sectors.

Seychelles Hospitality & Tourism Association (SHTA)

Tel: +248 432 5560 • Fax: +248 422 5718 • Website: www.shta.sc

The Seychelles Hospitality and Tourism Association was created in 2002 when the Seychelles Hotel Association merged with the Seychelles Hotel and Guesthouse Association. SHTA's primary focus is to unite all Seychelles tourism industry stakeholders under one association in order to be better prepared to defend the interest of the industry and its sustainability as the pillar of the country's economy.

International Coalition of Tourism Partners (ICTP)

Website: www.tourismpartners.org

ICTP is a travel and tourism coalition of global destinations committed to Quality Services and Green Growth.

International Institute for Peace through Tourism

Website: www.iipt.org

IIPT is dedicated to fostering tourism initiatives that contribute to international understanding and cooperation.

World Travel Market

WTM Africa - Cape Town in April, WTM Latin America - São Paulo in April, and WTM - London in November. WTM is the place to do business.

World Youth Student and Educational (WYSE) Travel Confederation

Website: www.wysetc.org

WYSE is a global not-for-profit membership organisation.

The Safari Awards

Website: www.safariawards.com

Safari Award finalists are amongst the top 3% in Africa and the winners are unquestionably the best.

World Luxury Hotel Awards

Website: www.luxuryhotelawards.com

World Luxury Hotel Awards is an international company that provides award recognition to the best hotels from all over the world.

Our December cover features Alfajiri Villas located in Diani on Kenya's South Coast, both of which are featured in this edition *(see our Destination story on pages 12 - 15, and Property Review on pages 18 - 21)*.

In this edition we also report on the Africa Travel Association's 40th Annual World Congress, which was convened in Nairobi, Kenya *(see page 16)*.

Whilst this edition focuses on Kenya, our regular content has not been ignored, which includes an opinion piece on the African Union's ill conceived funding model in the Business section *(page 06)*, and the latest tourism arrival and hospitality stats for South Africa *(page 08)*.

In the Conservation section, VulPro gets a helping hand from UK based The Hawking Centre *(page 11)*, and our legal beagle Louis the Lawyer continues his series on 'Enforcing your Contract' *(page 22)*.

And finally, our Marketing section provides sound advise for dealing with negative clients and colleagues *(page 23)*.

Looking back, 2015 has been a tough year for tourism in Africa. South Africa's total foreign arrival figures dropped by 7.1% in the first three quarters of the year as a direct result of Minister Malusi Gigaba's ill advised visa regulation fiasco, which cost the industry over R2,8 billion in lost revenue *(see Grant Thornton report on page 13 of our July edition)*. Although the visa regulations have subsequently been reviewed *(see page 06, November edition)*, it's going to take a while for the industry to recover.

Then there's the Ebola disease outbreak which blighted most of Western and Central Africa and wiped out four years of strong growth in Sub-Saharan Africa.

Despite these set backs, the hotel industry in Africa has seen significant expansion and seems to be set for a period of sustained growth. This is according to the Africa Hotel Investment Forum's projections for flight arrivals on-the-book (bookings for travel in future) from October 2015 to March 2016 running 4% ahead, compared with the same period last year *(see page 13, October edition)*.

According to South Africa's Minister of Tourism, Derek Hanekom, business tourism seems set for sustained growth. "The potential of Africa for the MICE industry is exponential. The tide has turned, we can see that our growth opportunities are now also within the African market. There are 770 registered African Associations on the ICCA database. 178 of these are based in South Africa and 592 on the rest of the continent and 218 regional conferences were registered on the continent in 2014 resulting in 610 events over the last five years. South Africa only hosted 63 of these events in the past 5 years" said Minister Hanekom.

Enjoy your reading and have a blessed festive season and a prosperous new year.

Des Langkilde.

editor@tourismtattler.com

The AU funding model, a threat to tourism in Africa

South Africa hosted the African Union Summit in Sandton in Johannesburg from 07 June 2015 to the 15 June 2015. The AU want all member countries to impose a US$2 hospitality levy per hotel stay and a US$10 airfare levy on each international flight entering or leaving Africa. This poses a significant threat to tourism in Africa, writes **Unathi Sonwabile Henama**.

The 25th African Union Summit occurred at a time when the AU is facing the reality that it cannot depend on donor funding in order to facilitate its future activities. The arrivals of heads of states, their support staff, media and other interested parties in South Africa was an opportunity for South Africa to benefit from business tourism. These tourists bring a much needed financial injection as they engage in tourism consumption that includes accommodation, shopping, travel and transportation and eating out at food and beverage outlets. Delegates attending a business tourism event such as the AU Summit are less price sensitive because the bulk of the expenses are paid for by the employer or sponsor of the delegates, which provides a substantial disposable income that can be used for shopping and other forms of tourism consumption. The delegates have an opportunity to see the beauty of South Africa and can in future return purely to come and consume destination South Africa as leisure tourists.

Efforts by the AU to raise its own funds independent of donors is imperative for the independence of the AU. It is of concern that the efforts of the AU to raise funding from member states has taken a decision that is detrimental to the tourism industry. The former Nigerian president, Olusegun Obasanjo was tasked by the AU to look for alternative sources of funding to enable AU member states to increase their share of the budget, with a view of relaxing dependence on donor funding. The Obasanjo report was adopted at the May 2013 AU Summit that approved that member countries must all impose a US$2 hospitality levy per hotel stay and a US$10 airfare levy on each international flight entering or leaving Africa. This is unfortunate as the AU is supposed to be funded by the treasury of each country instead of taxing the tourism industry to fund the AU. Africa receives less than 10% of global tourism receipts, which is practically a drop in the ocean when you consider the numbers of tourists that visit Europe and North America.

All countries in Africa have the ability to raise funds for their contribution to the AU if they ensure that there is appropriate governance. Governance and strong institutions for economic growth can assist a country to meet its obligations to its citizens and to continental bodies such as the AU. The poor levels of governance, and an array of failed states that lack accountability to their citizens has created the perennial African problem. The proposal of the Obasanjo report seeks to address the symptoms instead of the problems of the African countries being unable to pay their dues to the AU. In a paper by Peter Fabricius titled *'The AU starts to put its money* (closer to) *where its mouth is'*, it is noted that six countries namely Algeria, Angola, Egypt, Libya, Nigeria and South Africa would each pay 10% of member state's share of the AU budget. The resolutions taken at the 19th Session of the African Union from 15-16 July 2012, agreed on a US$5 cents levy per text message sent, US$ hospitality levy per stay in a hotel instead of a tourism levy and US$50 travel levy on flight tickets originating from or coming to Africa from outside Africa.

South Africa already has a tourism levy that is administered by the Tourism Business Council of South Africa (TBCSA) to market South Africa as a tourism destination. In terms of aviation, African countries must do more to liberalise international air transport services. The liberalisation of African air space can increase tourism revenues, create jobs and have a social benefit to society. The revenues from increased tourism can swell state coffers that could enable member countries to meet their commitments to the AU without adding new taxes on tourism and hospitality. The Yamousoukro Declaration that sought to accelerate air transport liberalisation in Africa must be fully implemented. In addition, member countries must not be shy to allow for domestic and international competition in their aviation sector, which would bring down prices and increase flight frequencies. Individual member countries in order to grow tourism must be bold enough to consider granting airlines the nine freedoms of the air to ensure a sustainable African aviation sector. In a paper titled Tourism in Africa: *'Harnessing Tourism for Growth and Improved Livelihoods'*, air transportation and accommodation are identified as a constraint to the development of tourism. The AU in the recent summit has picked up the new visa regulations are a concern for Africans seeking to travel to South Africa.

About the Author: Unathi Sonwabile Henama
teaches tourism in the Department of Tourism Management at the Tshwane University of Technology. The views expressed in this article are private. Unathi can be contacted via email at: HenamaUS@tut.ac.za or by calling: +27 (0)12 382 5507.

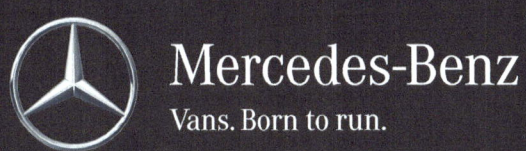

SATSA
Southern Africa Tourism Services Association

Grant Thornton

B✓NDED*

Market Intelligence Report

The information below was extracted from data available as at **08 December 2015**. By **Martin Jansen van Vuuren** of **Grant Thornton**.

ARRIVALS

The latest available data from **Statistics South Africa** is for **January to August 2015***:

	Current period	Change over same period last year
UK	255 863	0.1%
Germany	144 339	-9.8%
USA	193 394	-7.4%
India	52 099	-13.5%
China (incl Hong Kong)	48 136	-26.1%
Overseas Arrivals	1 315 243	-9.0%
African Arrivals	4 447 897	-6.6%
Total Foreign Arrivals	5 771 364	-7.1%

HOTEL STATS

The latest available data from **STR Global** is for **January** to **September 2015**:

Current period	Average Room Occupancy (ARO)	Average Room Rate (ARR)	Revenue Per Available Room (RevPAR)
All Hotels in SA	61.9%	R 1 057	R 654
All 5-star hotels in SA	61.3%	R 1 901	R 1 166
All 4-star hotels in SA	60.9%	R 1 000	R 609
All 3-star hotels in SA	62.0%	R 861	R 533
Change over same period last year			
All Hotels in SA	0.9%	5.9%	6.9%
All 5-star hotels in SA	0.3%	8.2%	8.5%
All 4-star hotels in SA	1.8%	5.2%	7.1%
All 3-star hotels in SA	-0.8%	6.2%	5.3%

ACSA DATA

The latest available data from **ACSA** is for **January to October 2015**:

Change over same period last year	Passengers arriving on International Flights	Passengers arriving on Regional Flights	Passengers arriving on Domestic Flights
OR Tambo International	-0.1%	-2.6%	9.1%
Cape Town International	9.7%	8.2%	7.9%
King Shaka International	-5.9%	N/A	5.1%

CAR RENTAL DATA

The latest available data from **SAVRALA** is for **January to June 2015**:

	Current period	Change over same period last year
Industry rental days	8 139 127	-1%
Industry utilisation	70.2%	-0.7%
Industry Average daily revenue	2 498 944 728	1%

WHAT THIS MEANS FOR MY BUSINESS

The Statistics South Africa data shows the negative impact of the visa regulations on international arrivals to South Africa. Hotel occupancies have been maintained, while rates increase off the back of the domestic tourism market as reflected in the growth in passengers arriving on domestic flights. *Note that African Arrivals plus Overseas Arrivals do not add to Total Foreign Arrivals due to the exclusion of unspecified arrivals, which could not be allocated to either African or Overseas. As from January 2014, Stats SA has stopped counting people transiting through SA as tourists. As a result of the revision, in order to compare the 2014 figures with 2013, it is necessary to deduct the transit figures from the 2013 totals.*

For more information contact Martin at Grant Thornton on +27 (0)21 417 8838 or visit: http://www.gt.co.za

we take care of your ~~shit!~~ admin

Sprout is a unique business consultancy whose vision is to assist tourism businesses in reaching their full potential through efficient business administration.

HR | MARKETING | ACCOUNTING | IT

info@sproutconsulting.co.za | www.sproutconsulting.co.za [f]

sprout CONSULTING
your outsourced head office

In Africa it is best to follow a leader.

The importance of having a specialist broker in Tourism and Leisure is undeniable. SATIB pioneered cover for this industry nearly 25 years ago and continues to stay ahead through innovation and regular consultations with clients and cover providers across Africa. Our established relationships with international and local insurers and our intimate understanding of the industry allows us to provide tailored products, ample capacity and exceptional services that ensure your business is secure. Make sure your Insurance Broker is in tune with your needs. Give us a call today and become one of our esteemed clients.

SATIB CONSERVATION TRUST
WILDLIFE & COMMUNITIES

For more information, please contact us on:
T 0861 SATIB 4U (72842 48) | **E** info@satib.co.za
www.satib.com

SATIB
Insurance Brokers

SATIB Insurance Brokers Pty (Ltd) is an authorised Financial Services Provider. FSP License No. 16388/ IGF No. 002366. Compliance Officer: National Compliance CC Practice No 1307

Competition

'Like' / 'Share' / 'Connect' with these Social Media icons to win!

The winning 'Like' or 'Share' during the month of **December 2015** will receive a **6-cup (800ml) Chrome Coffee Maker** with the compliments of **Livingstones Supply Co** – *Suppliers of the Finest Products to the Hospitality Industry*.

Livingston Supply Company

Tourism Tattler

Win

Competition Rules: Only one winner will be selected each month on a random selection draw basis. The prize winner will be notified via social media. The prize will be delivered by the sponsor to the winners postal address within South Africa. Should the winner reside outside of South Africa, delivery charges may be applicable. The prize may not be exchanged for cash.

Congratulations to our November Social Media winner

Winner

🐦 **@JenmanSafaris**

Jenman Safaris has been selected as our **November 2015** winner for their 'Follow' on **Twitter**. Jenman Safaris will receive a **Rainbow Nation Navigation Book + a hand crafted Leather Bracelet with red beading** with the compliments of **Livingstones Supply Co** – *Suppliers of the Finest Products to the Hospitality Industry*.

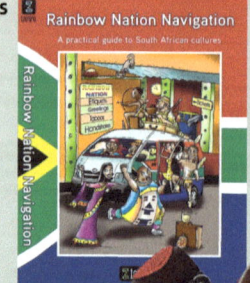

About the Prize from Livingstones Supply Co:

An abundance of cultures and 11 official languages makes interacting with South Africans very complicated. While you're wondering why someone behaves so strangely, they may be thinking the same thing about you! We need practical guidance to help us understand our diverse cultures, and 'Rainbow Nation Navigation' offers exactly that.

Price: R212.28 (R242.00 incl VAT)

For more information visit www.livingstonessupplyco.com

Vulture Saving Initiative Takes Flight

VulPro is proud to announce the launch of a funding partnership with UK based The Hawking Centre, writes **Kerri Wolter**.

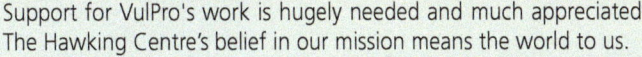

Support for VulPro's work is hugely needed and much appreciated. The Hawking Centre's belief in our mission means the world to us.

VulPro's mission is to advance knowledge, awareness and innovation in the conservation of wild African vulture populations for the benefit and well-being of society, and the charity is already involved in extremely valuable work in the fight to protect these incredible species.

VulPro is in fact working tirelessly to advance the conservation of South Africa's vultures, with a number of initiatives including adult and children education seminars and clubs, the captive breeding and release of vultures, rehabilitation, tracking and monitoring numbers of vultures in the wild as well as gathering vital information regarding the lesser known species such as the tree nesting vultures.

"The situation is approaching critical for SA vultures," says Jo Holmes of The Hawking Centre. "To date, the IUCN red list has listed the White Backed Vulture, Hooded Vulture and Rupell's Griffon Vulture as critically endangered, and the Cape Vulture, Lappet-Faced Vulture and White-Headed Vulture are listed as endangered. Action must be taken now to try and stop the overall decline in vulture populations, before it is too late; and this is why we have made our commitment to VulPro."

The Hawking Centre has pledged to support VulPro in both practical and financial ways. In addition to pledging regular funding through the company, our visitors will be made aware of the need for vulture conservation, and any donations made by visitors wishing to support VulPro will be passed on to the charity, free of any administration costs, and will attract a further pledge commitment from The Hawking Centre. Every client we welcome for their flying experience can have the satisfaction of knowing that their visit has had a direct effect on saving vulture populations in the wild.

In addition to funding, The Hawking Centre has pledged to help VulPro in practical ways, including funding the field visits of their employees to assist in hands-on vulture conservation, getting involved with programmes such as field monitoring and captive breeding initiatives, during annual one month field trips to Pretoria in South Africa.

Keep in touch with The Hawking Centre on facebook, twitter and through their blog to stay up to date with developments and progress made in vulture conservation.

Read more about VulPro and the amazing work they do at www.vulpro.com, or visit www.thehawkingcentre.co.uk

Diani Beach
Magical Kenya's
Hidden Gem

Kenya is renown as a Big 5 safari destination but not many are aware of its Marine 5, which abound along the country's 1420 km coastline. Here, some truly unique hidden gems await international tourists to show off its marine heritage. Diani Beach is a prime example of one of these gems, writes **Des Langkilde**.

The Marine 5 of course refers to the oceans Big 5; whales, giant manta rays, whale sharks, dolphins, and tiger sharks – all of which abound along the East Coast of Africa.

Diani is located 30 kilometres south of Mombasa, in Kwale County, which is named after its capital, although Ukunda is the largest town.

Diani's Golden Mile (the beach actually stretches for 6 miles, from the Kongo river to the north and Galu beach to the south - the southern point of reference is an old Baobab tree next to an ancient mosque alongside the Mwachema River), lies adjacent to Ukunda town and is bordered by an assortment of hotels, resorts and private villas that are accessed via the town's only tarred road.

This was my first trip to Kenya's South coast, although I had visited Kenya's Lamu Island on the North coast in 2014 (read the article here).

Arriving at Ukunda's airstrip onboard Safarilink's scheduled flight from Nairobi's Wilson Airport, our media group of five journalists were escorted to a waiting taxi by our able guide, Everlyne Partoip from Kenya Tourism Board (Everlyne also looks after KTB's social media, so needless to say that we were 'pushed to post').

After a short drive along a rutted sand road from the airport, and along Ukunda's singular tarred road, bordered by a miscellany of shanty structures interspersed with curio stalls, shopping centres and restaurants, our driver turned off the road following an obscure track beneath a liana strewn canopy of tropical forest. Our trepidation at arriving at an unmarked property access gate was soon dispelled as we were warmly welcomed by our Italian host Dr. Fabrizio Molinaro to, what we later discovered to be, the famous Alfajiri Villas. But that's another story – read our Property Review on page 00.

After a refreshing Safari Larger and late afternoon pizza snack, we retired to our respective villa rooms to change for a swim in the warm and tranquil Indian ocean swell of Diani Beach – a welcome relief after the dry bushlands of Mount Kenya (more on this trip in our January edition).

A walk along Diani Beach the following morning revealed that it is

not only the longest, but also the liveliest of Kenya's beaches with water sport activities that are as varied as they are ample. Kite surfing is popular, and local operators offer courses and equipment for sale or hire. Deep-sea fishing, glass-bottom boat trips, wind surfing, scuba diving, snorkelling and body boarding are just a few of the activities. The water is shallow near shore, with sandbars near the surface, which allow wading with a clear view of the sandy bottom, although sea urchins are an ever present threat. Adventure activities are also popular, such as sky diving or scenic flights up the coast in a microlight. For the less adventurous, camel rides are also offered along the beach.

A day excursion to Kisite Marine National Park, a 40 minute taxi drive to Shimoni along rutted sand roads to the south of Diani, is well worth the journey. Our media group arrived late, much to the disgruntled consternation of Pilli Pipa Dolphin Safari's owner Harm Lutjeboer, whose chastisement was fair considering that we'd held up the Dhow's scheduled 8:30am departure.

Pilli Pipa operate three Arab Dhows, all equipped with buoyancy jackets, cushioned seats, snorkelling and scuba diving equipment that includes optical prescription masks fitted with -3.00 to -7.00 lenses for nearsighted divers.

The marine park consists of four small islands surrounded by coral reef and is particularly suited to snorkelling with minimal current and clear visibility. Fishing and boat anchoring is prohibited in the marine park so the shallow reefs are in pristine condition. I've dived the reefs off neighbouring Tanzania's Zanzibar and Pemba islands, and Kisite's reefs compare favourably with sightings of triggerfish, moray eels, angelfish, wrasse, pufferfish, scorpionfish, damselfish, snapper, hawksbill turtles and dolphins. Apparently, over 45 types of coral and 360 fish species have been identified within the park.

The day excursion package includes a seafood lunch served with wine, beer and soft drinks on Wasini island. The fresh crab and filleted fish is prepared Swahili style, and the crisply fried seaweed is unusual and delectable.

Lunch is followed by an optional tour of the Shimoni Slave Cave. The slave cave is a haunting testament to the struggles of Africans who were enslaved by its invaders during the 18th and 19th century. The caves themselves have been formed by erosion from the rising and falling tide, and the walls are lined with metal studs and chains that were once used to bind and control the captive slaves. Slaves would be held in the caves for up to three weeks before boarding a Dhow to the slave market in Zanzibar before being shipped to Europe, Americas and Arabia.

There is also a Wasini Island mangrove boardwalk leading to the coral gardens, which is a community project maintained by the Wasini Women Group. Formed in 1978, the group works to identify and implement projects that will generate income for the village. The boardwalk takes you to excellent observation points to see the fossil coral gardens and mangroves, and you walk with an experienced and knowledgeable guide who explains the significance of the ecosystem, as well as mangrove species and significant coral formations.

Back at Diani, the nearby Shimba Hills National Reserve provides an opportunity for travellers to combine a safari with their beach holiday. The reserve is famous for being home to Kenya's only population of Sable antelope, also known as the Shimba Sable, and for the large elephant herds found there and in neighbouring Mwaluganje elephant sanctuary. The reserve is also an important site for birds, butterflies, and certain endangered species of cycad and orchids.

In conclusion, Diani is a hidden gem that ought to be included in Kenya inbound tour itineraries as it possesses a wide range of accommodation options to suit both budget and affluent travellers. The local tour operators and guides are professional and knowledgeable, and are keen to work with travel agents in structuring bespoke itineraries structured to meet the needs of leisure and niche tourism sectors.

For more information visit www.magicalkenya.com or www.ktb.go.ke

Magical Kenya

ATA's 40th Annual World Congress

I've attended travel trade conferences aplenty over the years, but ATA's World Congress has set the bar in terms of programme content and quality speakers, writes **Des Langkilde**.

KICC, Nairobi, Kenya

The Africa Travel Association (ATA) 40th Annual World Congress held in Nairobi, Kenya from 9 - 14 November, proved to be an eye opener.

The six day programme was certainly jam packed, kicking off with an optional pre-conference tour of Nairobi National Park and a visit to the David Sheldrick Wildlife Trust during the morning of day one. The afternoon consisted of a series of professional development breakout sessions built around topical plenaries, panels, and sessions convened at the Kenyatta International Convention Centre from 1:00pm through to 4:50pm. Delegates had the opportunity to choose between five marketing or five product development topics, which ran concurrently with each session lasting for 30 minutes. I kept jumping across to hear all 10 sessions lest I miss anything - talk about information overload!

For example, did you know that Kenya's Community Tourism sector is comprised of 38% Attractions, 26% Accommodation (Homestays & Community Lodges), and 32% Activities (camel walks, spilanking, etc). I guess the remaining 4% is uncategorised, but these were the stats divulged by the Director of Kenya Community Based Tourism Networks, Ole Taiko Lemayian.

In another session titled 'Maximising Media Exposure' speaker Juergen Thomas Steinmetz of eTurbo News explained how earning media is more economical than buying a string of ads. His assertion is that content marketing out performs conventional display advertising, and that destination marketing bodies are wasting their budget spend by contracting public relations companies to write press releases that never get published. It's far more economical, he said, to earn the publishers loyalty by splitting the budget spend between publishers and PR companies. I couldn't agree more!

I won't go into a blow-by-blow account of each day's programme (if you really want to see the full schedule with speakers click *here*). Suffice to say that each day was packed with insightful and useful information shared by carefully selected experts in their particular field of tourism expertise, a lot of which will be published in future editions of Tourism Tattler.

Most of the travel trade conferences that I've attended in the past average around 2.5 days in duration, but the six day ATA Congress format makes a lot more sense. Firstly, it allows time for off-site product visits to be included into the programme – in this regard the Kenya Tourism Board as the destination host did a sterling job. Secondly, the six day format provides more opportunities for delegates to network during tea and lunch breaks, at evening functions, and during off-site excursions – after all, networking is one of the major reasons that delegates register to attend.

In terms of networking, I was amazed that there were not more tour operators from other African countries in attendance. Considering that there were a large number of ATA member buyers from the USA and other key inbound markets to Africa, this Congress provided a perfect opportunity to meet them.

Notable in this regard is a comment made by one of ATA's USA outbound travel agent members, who said "After attending last years ATA Congress in Uganda and meeting the local tour operators who were present, I felt far more confident in doing business with them, especially in terms of doing bank transfers for booking deposits, and knowing that my clients will be in good hands when they arrive at their destination in Africa."

Overall, ATA's 40th Congress was a resounding success, and the Kenya Tourism Board did a sterling job in showcasing the country's tourism attractions, both during the event and in hosting of the 20 invited media journalists on post-event FAM trips.

The 41st ATA World Congress will be held in Rwanda during 2016, and Tourism Tattler will keep you informed on dates and registration links. See you there!

For more information visit www.africatravelassociation.org

H.E. Deputy President of Kenya, William Samoei arap Ruto, opening the ATA 40th Annual Congress.

The Fall and Rise of Tintswalo Atlantic

Tintswalo Atlantic was razed to the ground in March 2015 following a wildfire that blazed its way across the Cape Peninsula. Just three days shy of their eight-month rebuild deadline Tintswalo Atlantic re-opened to the public. This story shows what can be done when a team pulls together, writes **Kirsty Coetzee**.

On March 2nd, 2015, a wildfire that had blazed its way across the Cape Peninsula, was forced down the mountainside by strong winds, where it engulfed the Tintswalo Atlantic hotel and razed it to the ground. Tintswalo Lodges CFO, Gaye Corbett, recalls receiving a phone call in the early hours of that morning: "I don't know if you've ever had one of those middle-of-the-night phone calls, but it isn't a great experience. A million scenarios flashed through my head all at once."

There was little time for grief or remorse – the Tintswalo Lodge owners raced into action almost immediately. Tintswalo CEO, Warwick Goosen, caught the first flight to Cape Town to assess the damage on site, and to offer support to the Tintswalo Atlantic team and the surrounding community. Back in Johannesburg, co-owners, Lisa Goosen, and Gaye and Ernest Corbett, went to work with the reservations team to begin the arduous task of moving all future bookings to alternative hotels, before joining Warwick on site.

As the dust settled, the Tintswalo Lodges owners and Tintswalo Atlantic team brushed away their tears and rolled up their sleeves. It was quickly decided with determination and resolve that not only would they rebuild the hotel, but it would be completed within eight months and it would be better than before! Doubtful bystanders collectively rolled their eyes, declaring that a hotel could never be built that fast.

Little could the sceptics possibly fathom the passion that fuels the Tintswalo army! Joining forces with builder, Keith Rudd, who constructed the original Tintswalo Atlantic, and with Caroline Wright, Gaye Corbett's personal friend and interior decorator, and so many other contributing suppliers and community members, the formidable team set out to recreate paradise… and what a recreation they have achieved!

Launched on October 28th, just three days shy of their eight-month deadline, Tintswalo Atlantic re-opened to the public.

Addressing media and special guests at the first of four official launch parties, Gaye Corbett gave an account of the hurdles and triumphs of the past several months, saying, "The greatest challenge initially was just getting over the shock of losing the lodge. We had to get to grips with the fact that it was all gone and to somehow see the rebuild as an exciting challenge and not a complete loss, which is what it felt like after the fire. We realised that the only time you can truly and totally lose something is if you feel you can never recreate it again. When we had decided to go ahead, we put a deadline in place: and knew we'd stick to it. Once we had our building team in place, it was easy. Before we knew it, the job was done and now the lodge is back in all its glory!"

When asked if there were any alterations made to the design and layout of the hotel, Tintswalo owners admit that the fire has allowed them to correct small construction mistakes. And while the loss of the 300-year-old milkwood trees that had graced the lodge's decks will be felt for years to come, this also offered the opportunity to carefully select where to plant new younger trees. As a result, the hotel decks feel more spacious, and can better accommodate functions and al fresco dining.

As to the décor, Tintswalo Atlantic has retained its authentic spirit of charm and light and beauty; only it truly is better than it was before. Sourcing fabrics, artworks, small items, furniture and doors – literally from across the globe – has been a colossal task, admirably accomplished within an extremely limited timeframe.

Commenting on her personal highlight of the relaunch, Gaye expressed the satisfaction that she feels, knowing that the new hotel reflects and complements the unique beauty of its natural surroundings: "The eyes of the world were on us after the fire and when guests walk through the door now, the looks on their faces tell us that we have produced something that lives up to what we set out to achieve – a place of peace and beauty."

It's said that a person's true character comes to light when placed under extreme pressure. One could also say that this applies to an organization, which can be clearly seen by the way in which the Tintswalo staff, managers and owners have faced the odds with an enviable tenacity and an unbreakable attitude.

To experience this slice of heaven, contact the hotel directly at +2721 201 0025 / res1@tintswalo.com / www.tintswalo.com

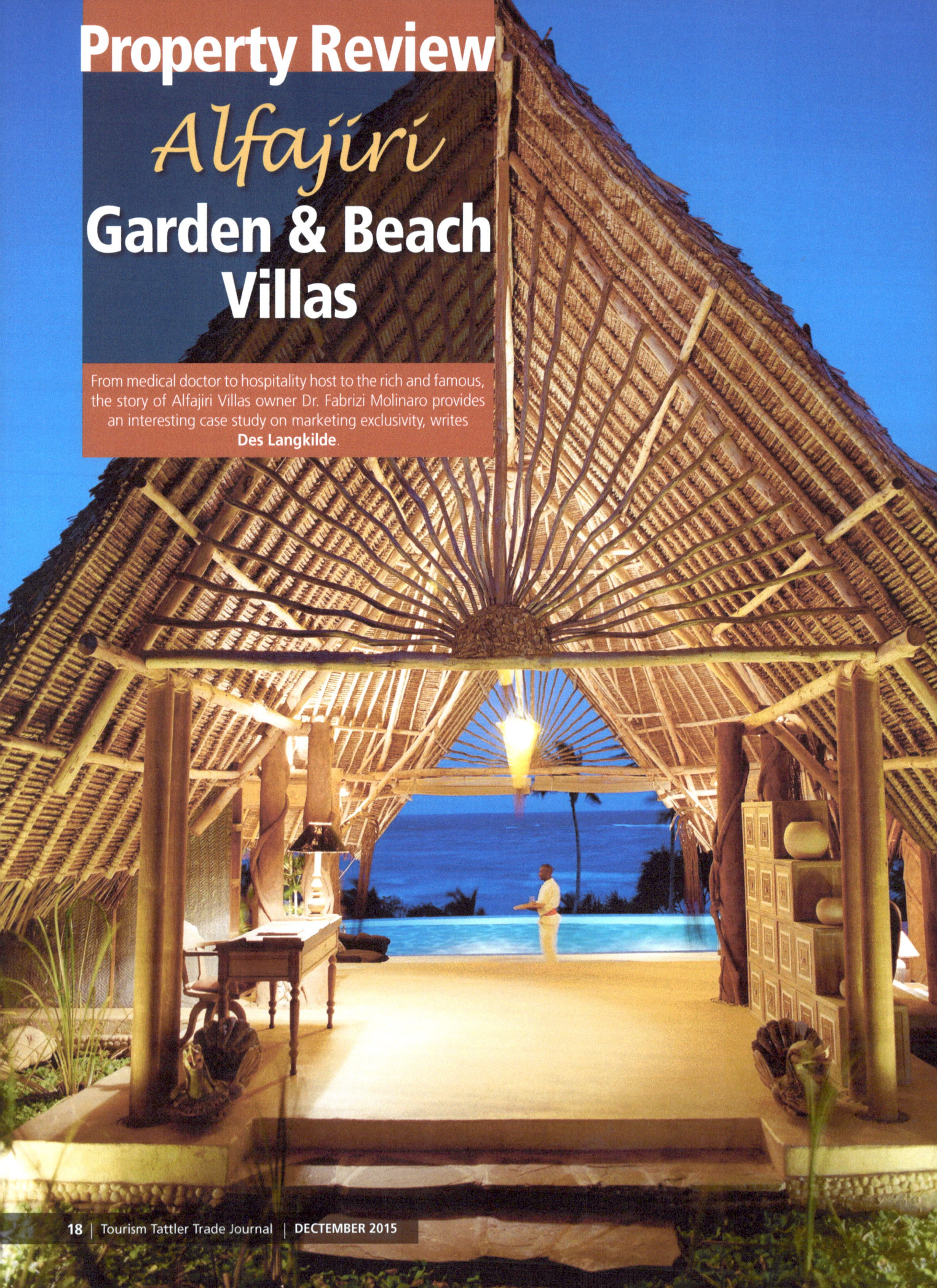

Property Review

Alfajiri

Garden & Beach Villas

From medical doctor to hospitality host to the rich and famous, the story of Alfajiri Villas owner Dr. Fabrizi Molinaro provides an interesting case study on marketing exclusivity, writes **Des Langkilde**.

Alfajiri, meaning 'dawn' in Swahili, is inappropriately named. I would have named it 'Mbinguni' (heaven) as the facilities and service offered here transcend the boundaries of mere mortal experience.

Alfajiri Villas is where the rich and famous come to hide from the paparazzi, relax in pampered privacy, and take leisurely strolls along Kenya's hidden coastal jewel – Diani Beach *(read our destination feature on page 00)*.

Rumour has it that this is where supercouple 'Brangelina' (Brad Pitt and Angelina Jolie) spent 5-nights in 2005 with Jolie's son Maddox, then 3. Alfajiri's owner Dr. Fabrizio Molinaro simply smiles knowingly when asked, but he does acknowledge that Rowan Atkinson was one of his first celebrity guests.

This photo of Brad Pitt and Angelina Jolie was taken on April 19, 2005 at Diani Beach, Kenya and confirmed the couple's relationship. Credit: Big Australia

Privacy is clearly an important factor to Alfajiri's reputation as a luxurious hideaway on the Kenya Coast, as no signage is evident anywhere along the only tarred road through Ukunda town.

"Alfajiri Villas can only be booked on an exclusive use basis, even in the case of 2 pax only, as each villa has its own private pool and private massage area," says Fabrizio.

This exclusivity comes at a price that befits its rich and famous status. $700 USD per person, per night covers your own villa with butler, private *a la carte* dining, served *al fresco* or in your villa – your choice, as is the choice of cuisine. All meals are included, as are all drinks, including local and imported brands of alcohol. Snorkelling and Gym facilities are available at a nearby resort and are also included, as are daily massages. A courtesy vehicle is also available for beach excursions or shopping in Ukunda.

So how did a medical doctor get to own and operate such a successful celebrity venue?

"I qualified as a doctor in Italy at the insistence of my father but never ended up practicing in that profession. At the time, military conscription was compulsory, so after completing my university degree, I accepted a one year contract as manager of a leading safari company in Kenya dealing with the Italian market – not so much to avoid the army, but I guess that was in the back of my mind at the time,' recalls Fabrizio.

"I fell in love with the African bush, with Kenya, and with my wife Marica – in that order. Marica is an interior designer and it was her passion that resulted in us purchasing our first property in Diani. As you know, Italians have very large extended families, and with our two daughters the original house became too small, so we built two villas with the same design: our Villa and then the Cliff Villa, which in the beginning we only used for friends and relatives. When the neighbouring property came up for sale, we bought it and built the Garden and Beach villas. We subsequently built Galdessa Safari ▶

Alfajiri

WATCH ▶ VIDEO

Alfajiri
BEACH VILLA
2:32 Minutes

Alfajiri
CLIFF VILLA
2:30 Minutes

Alfajiri
GARDEN VILLA
2:15 Minutes

Alfajiri

Camp in Tsavo East National park, so now offer both beach and bush experiences.

"When we opened Alfajiri in 2000, I already had 18 years experience in the hospitality business as I managed Intra Safaris limited, a DMC / safari company that was a leader in the Italian market, so we already knew a lot about personal service and what guests want when they take a holiday.

"The celebrity hosting reputation came about by default rather than planned intention. As with anyone, celebrities love to share their holiday experience with friends, and we soon started getting more bookings. Then word got around and we started getting bookings from their fans, who wanted to sleep in the same bed at their idol had," Fabrizio concludes with a knowing smile.

Each of the Alfajiri villas has its own distinctive charm and appeal:

The Cliff Villa caters for up to 8 guests accommodated in 4 bedrooms. Although the size and interior decor in the rooms are not the same, the Cliff Villa would not be suitable for 4 couples, but is ideal for families. The turret suite has a 270- degree view of the sea and must rate as one of the top five most romantic bedrooms ever.

Then there are two double rooms on the first floor, each with its own private veranda, and 1 twin room on the ground floor.

The Garden Villa can accommodate up to 10 guests in 4 large luxuriously appointed bedrooms (3 double rooms and 1 twin), each with its own large bathrooms, and all rooms overlook the Indian Ocean. All rooms are the same size but have different interior decoration, and is ideal for 4 couples travelling together.

The Beach Villa has 2 double rooms on the ground floor and 1 twin room on the first floor, each equipped with air conditioners and mosquito nets. An additional double room on the first floor is not air conditioned, but does have a fan and mosquito net. This villa is ideal for families with children or for honeymoon couples looking for the ultimate in privacy and service.

So, if there's anything to be learned from Fabrizio's experience it is this: host somebody with celebrity status, provide the best service possible, keep it secret and let the media speculate, then wait for his or her friends to book, knowing that their privacy is ensured. If only it were that simple!

For more information visit www.alfajirivillas.com

Legal

FROM THE BENCH™

With Louis the Lawyer
BENCHMARK ©

RISK IN TOURISM

– PART 16 –

THE LAW: CONTRACTS

REQUISITE #10: ENFORCING YOUR CONTRACT – PART 1

Homework – What To Do Before You Go Ahead

2. Have The Requisites Been Met? (Continued)

To recap where we ended off in Part 15 last month; The first question is has there been a clear and definitive offer and acceptance? The second question is whether the 'contract' the parties have entered into constitutes a legally binding obligation.

The third question that I want to cover here, is whether there is *consensus ad idem* i.e. have the parties actually agreed to the same thing/is there or has there been a *'meeting of the minds'*?

Sometimes when you look closely at the document that purports to be the binding contract, you will find that the parties *'where actually not on the same page'* and then a party may have to start the very tricky and expensive process of rectification relying on implied terms.

The way I prefer to draft agreements is based on the premise that (especially SME and SMME, of which there are many in the travel and tourism industry) not only do not have deep pockets but also don't have the time or patience to wait for a lengthy process during which more often than not much time is consumed by meeting after meeting, *'educating'* lawyers about the industry and ending up with 5, 6 or 7 draft agreements before actually arriving at wording that truly reflects the consensus of the parties!

So what I do is to say to the parties: "*You both understand your respective businesses and each others' better than I do (At least at the initial stage) so why don't you do the following: each of you go away and independently write down your expectations and deliverables; then meet and 'compare notes', combine same into the final agreed consensual document and submit it to me to ensure all legal requirements are met?*"

This process means the parties actually apply their minds and gives new meaning to the word 'N.E.E.D', which I treat as an acronym i.e. the parties need to ensure that each others' needs have been met and thus the acronym stands for: 'The Net Effect of Expectation & Delivery'!

However even if the contracting parties agree to that process there still remains one challenge: more often than not entrepreneurs don't have the patience and/or commercial reality may require that they (want to) start doing business immediately!

This is because by the time they arrive (in most instances) at the lawyer(s) ('Yes' there can be two and thus the education process and fees double up very quickly!) with all their notes, they've been talking for weeks and sometimes months and can't wait to start implementing their 'agreement'!

On the other hand my process often leads to the parties agreeing not to engage a 2nd lawyer, especially as I am well versed in the travel and tourism industry (with over 33 years' experience).

So, having said that, what they often do, despite having briefed an attorney(ies), is to start engaging in business based on one of the following: a handshake – a gentleman's agreement – a memorandum of understanding ('MOU'), heads of agreement ('HOA') or a letter of intent ('LOI').

Sadly, unless these documents are very meticulously drafted, they amount to no more than *'an agreement to agree'* which is NOT enforceable!

So I have created a *'bridging agreement'* known as a *'Letter of Commitment'* ('LOC').

The LOC is a two page agreement which contains the (initial) consensus and essential (albeit abbreviated) clauses re e.g. shareholding, funding, intellectual property, breach, dispute resolution and confidentiality, which is 100% enforceable and means the parties can start doing business immediately knowing that the legal requirements have been met.

And the cost?

A fraction of a lengthy 3 month/50 page document and peace of mind!

Being Positive When Your Colleagues Are Negative

Somehow no matter how much we may try to make December a happy month, there are always some people who tend to take a negative view on life. In a business environment, such as tourism, negativity can be deadly, writes **Dr. Peter E. Tarlow**.

It is essential that not only front line personnel maintain an upbeat view of the world, but also those who work behind the scenes. The basic rule is that negativity not only breeds further negativity but also tends to be self-serving in that negative and pessimistic people tend to create self-fulfilling prophecies.

Below are some suggestions on how to deal with negative people and turn negativity into positive actions:

Always set boundaries. It is not your responsibility to engage with a negative co-worker. Remind the person that you have to listen to customer complaints, but that no one is forced to work at this job and the option of seeking another job is always available. Let the complainer know that you are happy with your job and want to remain happy.

Avoid complainers. Chronic complainers are experts at turning creativity into failure and then blaming everyone but themselves. The best technique may be avoidance: smile, be polite but keep your distance.

Choose your battles. Tourism seems to breed complaints and it is not your job to fight every battle. Sometimes the best defence with an angry customer or co-worker is simply refuse to fight. The key is to realize that people who fight every battle become bitter and turn negative.

Beware of:

The can't wait to tell you the bad news person. These are the perhaps the most damaging of office people. They thrive not only on gossip but also more importantly on negative gossip. A good response is to inform the bearer of bad tidings that you would rather focus on the positive or on the solution rather than wallow in the negative. Turn the negative into positive actions by asking if there is something that you can do to improve the situation.

The Rumourmonger. Because tourism tends to be a volunteeristic activity, it is open to what may seem to be a never-ending series of rumours. Rumour spreaders love to tell us that the budget has been cut, that half the staff is to be fired, or that tourism receipts are reported to be down. Often these rumours are pure fabrications. When faced with rumours, ask for facts. Ask questions such as: who told you? How reliable is that person? A second solution is to point out that these types of rumours make you sick and that until facts are established you would prefer not to hear the rumour.

The eternal victims. Passengers often see themselves as victims, frontline personnel are often sure that they are victimized by both upper level management and by the tourist. People who are victims are never at fault, and the responsibility for a problem or crisis always belongs to another person. Try asking the person to tell you something positive. Even when dealing with an angry customer, see if you can turn a negative situation into a positive one by asking: so what was good about your experience? In the case of a co-worker who insists on being a victim, ask the person what he or she has learned from the situation and what she/he could have done better?

The over analyser. Negative people can sometimes behave irrationally and you can over analyse their actions and thus turn yourself into a gossip. In such cases give yourself a limited time to vent, say it and be done with it. When a person over analyses an issue, she/he wastes valuable time and energy. In most cases you will never make sense of the negative person's actions, so do not try! The key here as in all of tourism is do not become overly invested in an issue, empathize but do not sympathize.

Refuse to be negative but instead work at being positive. Tourism is all about fun, joy and a sense of *joie de vivre*. Do not allow others to bring you down. When you engage in negative thought or with negative people, you not only hurt yourself but you hurt the entire tourism industry. Experts in tourism know that both being positive and being negative are contagious. So be positive and your co-workers and customers will not only thank you but also begin to put a smile on their faces. The next time you feel yourself getting sucked into a negative black hole, refuse to enter and remember that tourism is all about getting the most out of life and in most cases it is about moments of unanticipated joy.

About the Author: Dr. Peter E. Tarlow publishes a monthly '*Tourism Tidbits*' newsletter. He is a founder of the Texas chapter of TTRA, President of *T&M*, and a popular author and speaker on tourism. Tarlow is a specialist in the areas of sociology of tourism, economic development, tourism safety and security. Tarlow speaks at governors' and state conferences on tourism and conducts seminars throughout the world. For more information e-mail *ptarlow@tourismandmore.com*